This book belongs to:

....

....

....

My first read-aloud
Bible

Retold by
Mary Batchelor &
Penny Boshoff

SCHOLASTIC INC.
New York Toronto London Auckland
Sydney Mexico City New Delhi Hong Kong

ABS logo trademark and copyright
American Bible Society, 1865 Broadway,
New York, NY 10023.

Published by Scholastic Inc. SCHOLASTIC
and associated logos are trademarks
and/or registered trademarks of
Scholastic Inc. All rights reserved.
12 11 10 9 8 7 6 5 4 3 2   13 14 15 16 17/0

Manufactured by CT Printing,
Shenzhen, China, in May 2013.
First printing, December 2009.

Contents

OLD TESTAMENT STORIES

Making our world

Long ago, when God
began to make
everything, the earth
was dark and empty.

God said, "Earth needs light."
And light appeared. God
made the sun to shine by
day and the moon and stars
to light the night.

God was pleased with what he had done.

God fills the world

God said, "I will make grass and flowers and trees to cover Earth."

Then he made all kinds of creatures.

He made fish to swim in the
rivers and seas. Birds and butterflies
to fill the air. And animals, big and
small, to play on the land.

Adam and Eve

God said, "Now I will make people to take care of the Earth." So he made Adam and Eve.

"Enjoy the fruit in my garden," said God.

Then he pointed to one tree. "Don't eat fruit from that tree. If you do, you will die."

Adam and Eve were very happy in God's garden.

Forbidden fruit

The fruit on the forbidden
tree looked delicious.
"Why not try it?"
the snake asked.
"But God said we would
die," said Eve.

"Don't listen to
God," the snake
whispered.

So Eve picked
some and
shared it
with Adam.
God was sad
that they had
disobeyed him.

Now Adam and
Eve had to leave
God's garden.

Genesis 3

15

Cain and Abel

Adam and Eve had two sons:
Cain and Abel. Cain thought that
God loved Abel more
than him. So he
hated his brother
more and more.

One day when they were out in the fields, Cain killed Abel.

God was very sad. Hate and murder were spoiling his Earth. Cain had to leave home and move far away.

Noah and the flood

Nobody on Earth listened to God—except Noah. "Noah, there's going to be a flood," said God.

"Build a big boat for your family. And take two of every kind of animal and bird with you."

Noah did what God told him. Then it rained and rained. Water covered the land. But Noah's boat floated safely.

Rainbow in the sky

At last the rain stopped. When the land was dry, Noah opened the door.

Out flew the birds. Off scampered the animals. And Noah said a special thank-you to God.

"Noah," said God, "when you see the rainbow, remember my promise: I will never flood the whole earth again."

God chooses Abraham

Abraham and Sarah longed
for a baby. One day God said,
"Abraham, I've chosen you.

"I will give you a new land
and a big family. Everyone in
the whole world will be happy
because of you and your family.

"So leave your house and take your tent. We're going on a journey."

Three strangers

One hot day Abraham
saw three tired strangers.
"Come and rest here!" he called.

So they sat in the shade
while Abraham brought them
food and water. He didn't guess
that they were God's messengers.

"Next year Sarah will have a baby
boy," they said.

Isaac

God kept his promise and
baby Isaac was born.

Some years later, God said, "Abraham, will you give Isaac back to me?"

But just as Abraham was getting ready to give Isaac back, God called out, "Abraham, I know now how much you love and trust me. I won't take Isaac away."

Genesis 22

27

Esau and Jacob

Isaac married Rebekah and they had twin sons: Esau and Jacob.

One day Esau arrived back from hunting. Jacob was cooking delicious food.

"Give me some!" cried Esau. "I'm starving!"
"Only if you give me your special place as eldest son," said Jacob.

"All right!" Esau agreed.

Jacob's dream

Jacob tricked Esau again.
Esau wanted to kill Jacob.
So Jacob ran away.

That night Jacob slept
under the stars.

In his dream he saw a staircase. Angels were going up and down.

Then God said, "Jacob, I promise to be with you. I'll never leave you. You and your family will have the good things I promised to Abraham."

Joseph's coat

Jacob had lots of children but Joseph was his favorite. He gave Joseph a beautiful coat. Joseph's brothers were jealous.

One day Joseph went to the fields to find his brothers.

"Let's get him," the brothers cried. They grabbed Joseph, ripped off his special coat, and threw him down an empty well.

Joseph goes to Egypt

The brothers decided to sell Joseph to some men traveling to Egypt.

In Egypt, Joseph became Potiphar's slave.

Because Joseph worked so hard, Potiphar put him in charge of everything he had.

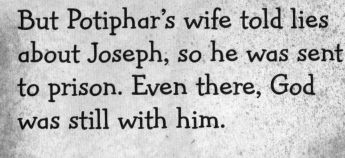

But Potiphar's wife told lies about Joseph, so he was sent to prison. Even there, God was still with him.

Joseph saves Egypt

The king of Egypt had worrying dreams. "Fetch Joseph," a servant said. "He understands dreams."

The king told Joseph his dream. "God says seven good harvests are coming, followed by seven bad ones," Joseph explained. "Save food now to feed your people in the bad years."

The king was pleased. "Joseph, you must help me lead Egypt."

Brothers reunited

Now Joseph's brothers had to travel to Egypt to buy corn. They did not know that the man in charge was Joseph. Joseph pretended to be angry.

Then he said, "Don't be frightened.
It's me, Joseph! I will take care of you.
God brought me here to save everyone!
Come and live
in Egypt."

Moses

God gave Jacob the name "Israel." Israel's people stayed in Egypt. But years later, a cruel king made them his slaves.

"Kill all their baby boys!" he ordered. But one mother hid her baby in a floating basket among the river reeds.

"What's in that basket?" asked the princess. Her servant opened the lid.

"What a beautiful baby!" the princess exclaimed. "I shall keep him and name him Moses."

Fire in the bush

When Moses grew up he longed to save his people. The king was furious, so Moses ran far away.

One day, Moses saw a bush on fire. "That's strange!" he thought.

Suddenly God spoke from the bush.
"Moses, go back to Egypt
and rescue your
unhappy people."

"I can't!" Moses exclaimed.
"Yes, you can," God said,
"because I will be with you."

Moses warns the king

Moses set off for Egypt.
"God says you must let his
people go," he told the king.

"NO!" the king replied. "I don't know or care about your God. I won't let them go. Make the Israelites work harder!"

"Obey God or bad things will happen," Moses warned.

"I won't!" the king replied.

Exodus 4, 5

45

Chaos in Egypt

Everything happened as Moses had warned. First frogs ran everywhere, then flies came, then there were storms.

But still the king would not let the Israelites go.

"God will rescue his people," Moses said,
"but because of you, Egypt will be sad."
"Go away!" the king shouted.

"Tomorrow God will rescue us,"
Moses told the Israelites.
"Cook a special meal to thank him."

Exodus 4–12

47

The waves roll back

The next day the Israelites left Egypt and camped by the Red Sea. But the Egyptian army chased them!

God said, "Moses, stretch your stick over the sea. Tell the people to go forward."

Moses obeyed God.
The waters rolled
back and the Israelites
crossed on dry ground.

"Hurrah!" they shouted on the
other side. "God has rescued us!"

Exodus 13–15

God sends food

"God is leading us to the country he promised us," Moses told the Israelites as they walked through the desert.

"There's nothing to eat!"
the people grumbled.

"I will feed you every day," God promised.

The next morning the ground was
covered with small white flakes.
They tasted good, like honey biscuits.

God gives water

The people kept grumbling. "We're thirsty, Moses," they moaned. "Give us water!"

Moses told God and God said, "Go to the special rock that I will show you and hit it with your stick."

Moses did as God told him and cool, refreshing water gushed from the rock. There was plenty for everyone.

Rules for the people

God said to Moses, "These rules will help my people every day: Put me first and love me best. Don't worship anyone but me. Don't use my name carelessly. Keep one day each week as a resting day with me.

"Obey your father and mother. Don't hurt others. Keep love between a husband and wife special. Don't take what isn't yours. Don't tell lies about other people. Don't be jealous of other people and want what they have."

Reaching Canaan

When they reached the land God had promised them, Moses sent twelve spies to look around.

"It's a wonderful country," the spies said, "but we'll never win it! The people there are huge and strong!" But Caleb and Joshua shouted out, "Don't cry! God will help us win!"

Brave Rahab

When Moses died, God made Joshua
the leader. Joshua sent two
spies to Jericho.

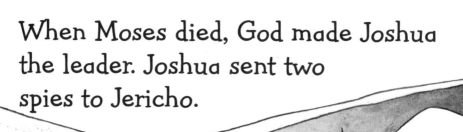

The king sent soldiers
to seize them, but Rahab
hid them.

Finally the soldiers left.

Rahab said to the spies:
"When God gives you Jericho,
please be kind to me."
"We will!" they promised.

Joshua 1, 2

59

The walls fall down

Joshua did everything God told him.

So for six days Joshua and the soldiers
and priests marched once around Jericho.
On the seventh day they marched around
seven times, blowing their trumpets.

Then everyone shouted. At once the
walls of the city fell. CRASH! But Rahab
was not hurt.

Gideon

The Israelites soon forgot God.
But God did not forget them.

When enemies attacked Israel, God said
to Gideon, "Rescue my people. I'll show
you how!"

That night Gideon and his soldiers crept
to the enemy camp with trumpets and jars
with torches inside.

At Gideon's signal, every
soldier smashed his jar,
blew his trumpet, and
shouted, "For God and for Gideon!"
And Israel's enemies ran away!

Samson's riddle

More enemies attacked Israel.
This time God chose strong
Samson to fight them.

Samson told his enemies
this riddle:

"Out of the eater came something to eat.
Out of the strong came something sweet."

His enemies, the Philistines, were puzzled.
Then they discovered that Samson had
found a bee's nest in a lion's dead body
and he'd eaten the delicious honey.

Samson and the Philistines

Finally the Philistines caught Samson. They blinded him and brought him to their temple. "Our god Dagon is the greatest!" they shouted.

"God, please help me to beat the Philistines," Samson prayed.

He put his hands on the big pillars and pushed and pushed. Crack. CRASH! The temple fell down and killed everyone. Samson was remembered as a great hero.

Naomi and Ruth

Naomi's family lived in Bethlehem. But when the food ran out, they moved to far-away Moab.

Poor Naomi! Her husband and sons died. But their Moabite wives, Orpah and Ruth, looked after her.

"I'm going back to Bethlehem," Naomi said.
"Good-bye," said Orpah, hugging Naomi.

But Ruth said, "I'm coming with you.
I'll stay with you always. I love you
and your God will be my God."

A happy ending

Naomi and Ruth arrived in Bethlehem. They were so poor that Ruth picked up leftover grain from the fields to make bread.

"Who's that stranger?" asked the farmer Boaz.

"That's Ruth. She takes good care of Naomi," the farmworkers replied. "Then drop extra grain for Ruth," Boaz said kindly. Boaz decided to marry Ruth.

They soon had a little boy. Now Naomi was very happy.

Ruth 2–4

God answers a prayer

Hannah longed for a baby!

One day, she visited God's house with her husband. Hannah felt so sad.

"Please God," she cried, "send me a baby.
I promise I'll give him back to you."

Eli, the priest, heard her.
"May God answer your prayer!" he said.
And God did!

Hannah called her baby Samuel.

God calls Samuel

Hannah kept her promise.
She took Samuel to live
with Eli, the priest,
at God's house.

One night, Samuel
heard a voice:
"Samuel!"
He ran to Eli.
"I didn't call,"
Eli said.
"Go back
to bed."

Three times Samuel heard the voice and three times he ran to Eli.

Then Eli said, "It's God's voice. Next time he calls, say, 'I'm listening.' "

God called again and Samuel listened to God's message.

King of Israel

Samuel gave God's messages to the Israelites. But they wanted a king instead. "I will choose their king," God told Samuel.

One day a young man called Saul arrived. "My father's donkeys ran away," he told Samuel.

"I can't find them anywhere. Can you help me?"

"Don't worry, your donkeys have been found," Samuel said. "God has chosen you to be king of Israel!"

1 Samuel 8–10

Saul disobeys God

One day the Israelites were getting ready for battle.

"Wait for me to pray before you fight," Samuel told King Saul.

King Saul waited and waited. Finally, he decided to say the prayers himself. Just then Samuel came back.

"Why didn't you wait?" Samuel asked sadly. "Because you won't obey God, he is going to choose another king."

A new king

"Go and see Jesse," God told Samuel. "I have chosen one of his sons to be king." Jesse's eldest son was handsome.

"He looks like a king!" thought Samuel. But God whispered, "No! Not this one."

Samuel saw six more sons.
But each time God said, "No!"
"Have you another son?"
Samuel asked.
"Only young
David," Jesse
replied. "He's
looking after
my sheep."

When David arrived, God told
Samuel, "He is the one! My chosen king!"

David and Goliath

David's brothers were in Saul's army. David was visiting them when the huge Philistine soldier, Goliath, bellowed, "Israelites, choose a man to fight me!"

The Israelites were terrified.

"I'll fight him!" said David, taking just his shepherd's sling and five stones. "I'll feed you to the birds!" roared Goliath. "I fight with God's strength!" David shouted. He aimed. The stone from his sling hit Goliath's skull . . . crack!

Goliath crashed to the ground.

David and Jonathan

Saul invited David to live in his palace. Whenever Saul was miserable, David would sing and play his harp to cheer him up.

David and Jonathan, Saul's son, became great friends.

But Saul grew jealous of David.

84

One day Saul hurled his spear at David. David dodged just in time!

"Go," said Jonathan, "or my father will kill you!"

The two friends hugged each other and sadly said, "Good-bye."

1 Samuel 16, 18, 19

85

Saul chases David

When Saul discovered David had gone, he chased him.

One night David and his nephew, Abishai, crept up on Saul and his soldiers as they slept. "Kill Saul now!" Abishai whispered.

"Never!" David replied. "God would not want that. We'll take Saul's spear and water jug instead!"

When Saul discovered that David had taken his spear and jug but had not hurt him, he promised to stop chasing David.

David becomes king

One day Saul and Jonathan died in battle and David became king.

"Jonathan is dead," David said sadly. "I must look after his family." "Then take care of his son Mephibosheth," a servant said. "He can't walk."

So David invited Jonathan's son to the palace. "Welcome, Mephibosheth," he said.

"Come and live here and have dinner with me every day."

Wise Solomon

When David died, his son Solomon became king. Solomon asked God to help him rule well. God made him wise.

One day two mothers arrived with a baby. "He's my baby!" the first woman cried.

"No! He's mine," the other shouted.
"Cut the baby in two,"ordered
Solomon, "and give each
mother half!"
"No!" cried the first
woman. "Don't
hurt him! Let her
have him!"

"Take the baby," Solomon told the first
woman, "for you are the real mother."

A temple for God

God made Solomon rich as well as wise. Solomon began to build a splendid home for God—the temple.

Thousands of builders got busy with fine wood and huge stones. Inside, in God's special room, even the floor was paved with gold!

Finally it was finished.
Everyone celebrated.

God promised to listen to his people when they prayed to him there.

Elijah and the bad king

Some kings of Israel were bad. King Ahab and his wicked queen, Jezebel, prayed to false gods and killed many of God's friends.

One day God's friend Elijah brought Ahab a message. "I serve the true God. There will be no rain until I say so!"

What Elijah said came true. Plants and animals began to die. Everyone was hungry. But God looked after Elijah.

The real God

"Bring the servants of the false god Baal to Mount Carmel," Elijah told Ahab. "We'll prove who's the real God."

"Build a fire with wood," Elijah told Baal's followers. "Now ask Baal to light it."

They prayed and prayed but nothing happened!

Elijah poured water over his wood. Then he prayed: "Please, God, send fire!" At once, fire streaked down and set Elijah's wood alight. "Our God is the real God!" shouted the Israelites.

1 Kings 18

97

Elijah and Elisha

Jezebel was furious. She wanted to kill Elijah. But God kept him safe.

"Find Elisha," God told Elijah. "He'll help you. He will be my messenger too."

One day Elijah and Elisha were walking together, when they heard a rushing noise. Suddenly a chariot of fire, drawn by fiery horses, swooped down between them.

A great wind whirled Elijah off his feet. He was lifted up, up, and away— until Elisha could see him no more.

One bottle of oil

A widow came to Elisha. "Help me!" she sobbed. "They're taking my sons away because I owe money."

"What have you got at home?" Elisha asked. "One small bottle of oil," she said.

"Borrow lots more bottles and fill them with your oil," Elisha said.

The boys fetched bottles and their mother poured and poured . . .

The oil didn't run out until every borrowed bottle was full! "Now sell the oil to pay your debt," said kind Elisha.

Naaman is healed

Naaman, chief of the Syrian army, had a terrible skin disease. His young Israelite servant girl said, "Go to Elisha—God's messenger in Israel—he will make you better."

"Wash seven times in the river Jordan," Elisha told Naaman. "I can wash in cleaner rivers back home!" Naaman shouted angrily.

"Please do as Elisha says!" his soldiers pleaded. So Naaman dipped in the river seven times—and his skin was smooth again!

"Your God is the real God!" Naaman told Elisha.

King Joash

After King Ahaziah died, his mother Athaliah killed all the royal children to become queen!

But baby Joash was rescued by his aunt. She hid him in God's temple.

When Joash was seven, the priest, Jehoiada, invited the people to the temple. He led Joash out, placed a crown on his head, and gave him a copy of God's Law. Everyone cheered, "Long live King Joash!"

Athaliah was furious.
Now Joash was God's king.

Jonah and the big fish

God told Jonah, "Go to the people of Nineveh. Tell them to stop being wicked." Jonah didn't want to go. He ran away and went to sea.

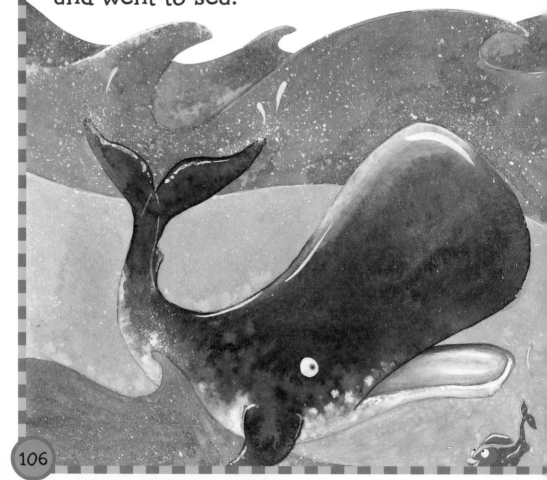

But God sent a strong wind to whip up the waves. "We're going to sink!" cried the terrified sailors.

"It's my fault!" Jonah said. "I ran away from God. Throw me in the sea, then the storm will stop." The sailors threw Jonah overboard and the sea grew calm.

Jonah 1

God forgives

As Jonah sank beneath the waves, a big fish swam by and swallowed him up.

Inside the fish Jonah prayed, "Please help me, God!"
God listened. He told the fish to spit Jonah out on the beach.

So Jonah went to Nineveh. The people listened to him. They promised to stop being wicked.

"I forgive them," God told Jonah. But Jonah was angry. He did not want God to forgive his enemies.

A lost book is found

God's temple in Jerusalem was falling to bits, so King Josiah sent builders and decorators to mend it.

There they found the lost copy of God's Law. A servant read it to King Josiah. He burst into tears.

"We haven't obeyed God!" he cried.

God sent Josiah a message: "There will be trouble later, but not for you, Josiah. I know you love me!"

2 Chronicles 34

Jeremiah is rescued

After good King Josiah there were more bad kings. God's messenger, Jeremiah, warned them that their enemies would fight them and win if they kept disobeying God.

The leaders got angry— they threw Jeremiah into a deep, muddy hole.

Ebedmelech went to the king.
"Your Majesty! Don't let Jeremiah die!"
"Go and rescue him!" ordered the king.

So Ebedmelech and his helpers rushed
off to pull Jeremiah up to safety.

Leaving Jerusalem

No one listened to Jeremiah's messages from God.

Then Nebuchadnezzar—mighty king of Babylonia—brought his army to attack Jerusalem.

They stole the temple treasure and marched the people off to Babylonia.

"Burn the city!" Nebuchadnezzar ordered. How sad God's people were as they left the city and the land God had given them!

Daniel

Israel's cleverest young men were taken to Nebuchadnezzar's palace.

"Eat the food the king sends you," the chief servant ordered. But Daniel, Shadrach, Meshach, and Abednego knew that meant obeying the king rather than God.

"Give us vegetables and water for ten days," Daniel begged. The servant agreed.

After ten days they looked fit and healthy. "These men are the best!" Nebuchadnezzar said. "They will help me rule."

Saved from the fire

"Bow down to my wonderful gold statue!" Nebuchadnezzar ordered.

Everyone bowed down—except Shadrach, Meshach, and Abednego.

"Bow down!" Nebuchadnezzar shouted. "Or I'll throw you into the fire!"

"We bow only to God!" the friends replied bravely. So Nebuchadnezzar's soldiers threw them into the flames.

Suddenly Nebuchadnezzar gasped: "We threw three men in—but there are four walking about in the fire! Their God has sent his angel to keep them safe!"

Daniel 3

Daniel and the lions

The new king liked Daniel. This made people jealous. "Order everyone to pray to you alone—or be thrown to the lions," they told the king.

"Daniel is still praying to God!" said his enemies. So the king's soldiers threw Daniel into the lions' pit.

The king lay awake worrying. Next morning he shouted, "Daniel! Did God save you?"

"Yes!" Daniel replied. "My God closed the lions' mouths! I'm safe!"

Queen Esther

"I want a queen," said the king of Persia. "Bring me the most beautiful girls in the kingdom."

The king chose Esther. But he did not know that Esther and her cousin Mordecai were Jews.

Haman hated Mordecai, so he said to the king, "Let's kill those Jews from Israel."

The king agreed.

Mordecai sent Esther a secret message: "Help us!" he begged. "God made you queen to save your people."

Esther saves the Jews

"I will help," Esther told Mordecai.
"Pray that the king will not
be angry!"

Then, trembling, she went to the king.
He welcomed her.

"Please come to dinner—and bring Haman, your chief advisor," Esther said.

After dinner Esther said, "Your Majesty, an enemy wants to kill me and my people!"

"Who is he?" the king asked. Esther pointed to Haman.

"Take him away!" the king ordered. "Mordecai will take his place."

Rebuilding Jerusalem

After many years, the Jewish people came home, just as God had promised.

Jerusalem was in ruins.
So the people began
rebuilding the temple.

Ezra, the priest, helped them finish
it and taught them God's Word.

"Now let's rebuild the city wall,"
said Nehemiah. "God will help us!"
So the people worked together, each
family mending a part of the wall.

Give thanks to God

At last the wall was finished! Nehemiah called everyone to celebrate.

Two groups of singers and musicians marched right around Jerusalem.

The people sang, played their instruments, danced, and thanked God.

They all met up again at the temple. Everyone was happy because God had kept his promise.

The people of Israel had come home!

Nehemiah 6, 12

NEW TESTAMENT STORIES

An angel visits Mary

One day God sent the angel
Gabriel to see Mary.

"Mary, don't be afraid,
God is pleased with you,"
Gabriel said. "You are
going to have a baby.
Call him Jesus.
He will be a
great king."

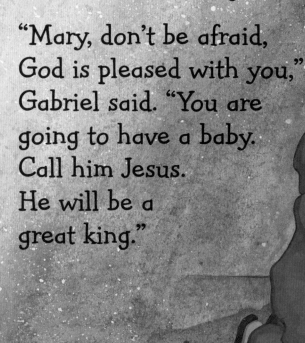

Mary looked puzzled.
"The baby will be God's
Son," Gabriel explained.
"I will do whatever God
wants," Mary replied.

Mary visits Elizabeth

Mary couldn't wait to tell her cousin Elizabeth the news. She left home and hurried off.

"Elizabeth!" she called, running to the house.

Elizabeth hugged her.
"Mary! How wonderful! As soon
as I heard you I knew that God had
chosen you to be the mother of his
promised king!"

Mary was so happy she sang
"thank you" to God.

A special message

Joseph wanted to marry Mary. When he heard about Mary's baby he was worried.

That night, God's angel gave Joseph a special message.

"Joseph, don't worry!" the angel said.
"God wants you to marry Mary."

"Her baby has been made by
God's Holy Spirit. Call him Jesus.
One day he will rescue God's people."

So Joseph married Mary.

Jesus is born

Bethlehem was busy. Mary
and Joseph had traveled all
the way from Nazareth.
They needed somewhere
to sleep, but all
the inns
were full.

At last Joseph found somewhere
warm and dry—a stable!

That night, Jesus was born.
Mary wrapped him up warmly
and laid him to sleep in the hay.

Luke 2

The shepherds

Shepherds were looking after their sheep when an angel appeared. God's dazzling light shone around.

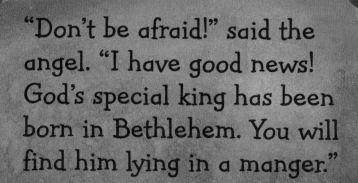

"Don't be afraid!" said the angel. "I have good news! God's special king has been born in Bethlehem. You will find him lying in a manger."

Suddenly, the sky was filled with angels singing to God.

The shepherds ran to Bethlehem. They were so happy when they found Jesus!

A promise fulfilled

One day Mary and Joseph
took baby Jesus
to the temple.

There they
met an old man
called Simeon.

Simeon had loved God all his life.
He took Jesus gently in his arms.
"I'm so happy today!" he said. "Thank
you, God, for keeping your promise and
letting me see
the king who
will rescue
us all."

The wise men

Far away in the East, some wise
men saw a bright new star.
"How wonderful!" they cried. "A great king
has been born! Let's go and worship him!"

So they followed the
star until it stopped over
a house in Bethlehem.

The wise men were so happy to see Jesus. They bowed down low and gave him precious gifts—gold, frankincense, and myrrh.

Leaving for Egypt

After the wise men had gone, Joseph saw an angel in his dreams.

"Joseph! Get up!" said the angel. "Hurry! Cruel King Herod wants to hurt Jesus. Go to Egypt. You will all be safe there. I will tell you when to come back."

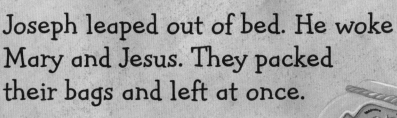

Joseph leaped out of bed. He woke Mary and Jesus. They packed their bags and left at once.

After King Herod died, an angel told Joseph it was safe to return home.

Jesus in the temple

Mary, Joseph, and Jesus had been worshiping God in Jerusalem. They were traveling home to Nazareth.

"Have you seen Jesus?" Mary asked. Joseph shook his head. Oh no! Jesus had been left behind.

Mary and Joseph rushed back to Jerusalem. They found Jesus in the temple.

"I've been here in my Father's house," said Jesus.

John baptizes Jesus

"Come back to God!" John shouted. "Say you are sorry and get baptized in the water so that God will forgive you and make you clean inside and out!"

The people did what John told them.

Jesus was good. But he came to be baptized too. He always did what God wanted.

When Jesus came out
of the water, God said,
"You are my own dear Son.
I am pleased with you!"

A test for Jesus

Jesus went into the desert to get ready to do God's work. God's enemy, the devil, came to trick Jesus.

"I'll give you the whole world, if you bow down to me," he said.

"No!" said Jesus. "God has told everyone to bow down and serve no one else but him."

Jesus chose to listen to God, not the devil, so the devil left.

Andrew meets Jesus

One day, Andrew and
his friend followed Jesus.

"Where do
you live?"
Andrew called
out. "Come
and see!"
said Jesus.

So they went to Jesus' house and talked with him all afternoon.

Then Andrew rushed to find his brother. "Peter!" he said, "Come and meet Jesus, he's the king God promised us!"

Peter goes fishing

Jesus was at the lake telling people about God. He climbed into Peter's boat. "Let's go fishing!" he said.

"I've been fishing. I didn't catch *anything*!" Peter replied. But he did what Jesus said.

Suddenly the nets were bursting with wriggling fish. Peter was amazed.

"Peter, come with
me and we'll go
fishing for people!"
Jesus said.
So Peter left
his boat and
followed Jesus.

Water into wine

Mary and Jesus were at a wedding. Mary was worried. "Jesus, there's no more wine!"

"Fill these big jars with water," Jesus told the servants.

"Then give some to the man in charge."

When the servants did what Jesus told them, they were amazed. Jesus had turned ordinary water into the very best wine!

Walking again

"Jesus will help you walk again,"
said the men as they carried their
friend to Jesus' house.

The house was too crowded.
So they dug a hole in the roof
and lowered their friend down.

Jesus smiled and said to the man,
"I forgive you. Now get up and walk home!"

To everyone's
amazement, the
man stood up and
began to walk!

Mark 2

A wise man and a foolish man

One day Jesus told a story:

There was once a foolish man who built his house on the sand. But the wise man built his house on the rock.

The wind shook the houses. The rain poured down, the floods rose. The house on the sand fell . . . CRASH! But the wise man was safe.

"If you do what I tell you," said Jesus, "you will be safe too!"

The trusting soldier

An important soldier came to Jesus.
"My servant is very ill!" he said.

"I'll come and make him well," said Jesus.

"You don't need to come to my house," the soldier said. "Just give the order and my servant will get better."

"I'm pleased you trust me so much!" said Jesus. "Go home, your servant is well now."

Buried treasure

"When you find God's kingdom, you will never let it go," Jesus said to his friends. And he told them this story:

A man was digging in a field when he found treasure.

"If I buy this field, the treasure will be mine!" he thought.

So he sold everything he had. Then he bought the field. He was so happy—now the treasure was his forever!

The story of the seeds

"If you listen to me," said Jesus, "you'll be like the good soil in this story."

A farmer sowed his seeds.
Some seeds fell on the path.
The birds gobbled them up.

The seeds among the stones grew quickly but they dried up in the hot sun.

Other seeds grew well until the weeds got in their way.

The seeds on the good soil grew into tall, healthy plants.

Jesus calms the storm

It had been a busy day. Jesus was fast asleep in his friends' boat.

Suddenly a wild wind whipped up the waves. They came crashing over the boat.

"Wake up, Jesus!" his friends shouted. "The boat is sinking!"

Jesus got up. "Waves! Calm down!" He ordered, "Wind, be quiet!"

At once all was safe and still. Jesus' friends were amazed. "Even the wind and waves do what Jesus says!"

The sick girl

Jairus' daughter was very ill. "Jesus, please make her better!" he begged.

Just then his servant ran up. "Your daughter is dead," he said sadly.

"Trust me, Jairus," Jesus said gently, "your little girl will get well."

At Jairus' house everyone was crying. The girl was lying pale and still.

"Little girl," Jesus said, taking her hand, "get up!" She opened her eyes and stood up—alive and well.

Jesus and the blind men

As Jesus left Jairus' house two blind men shouted out, "Jesus, be kind and help us!"

"Do you believe I can make you better?" Jesus asked. "Oh yes!" they replied.

"Then because you believe in me, it will happen," said Jesus as he reached out and touched their eyes.

At once the men could see!

Food for everyone

The crowd had listened to Jesus all day.

"They're hungry," said Jesus. "Let's give them some food."

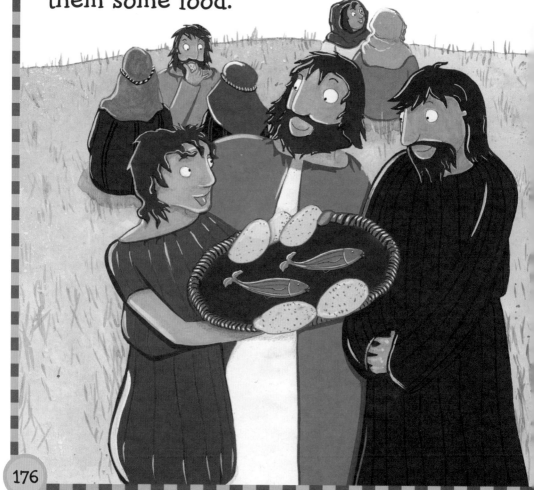

"We don't have enough money!" his friends replied. "This boy has five little loaves and two fish," said Andrew. Jesus took the loaves and the fish and thanked God for them.

Then he handed out the food. And everyone had plenty to eat!

Jesus walks on water

One evening Jesus went away to pray.
His friends set off across the lake.
They puffed and panted as they rowed.

Suddenly they saw someone walking
on the water toward them.
"It's a ghost!" they screamed.

"Don't be scared," said the man,
climbing into their boat. "It's me, Jesus!"
The friends were amazed. It *was* Jesus!

Mark 6

God talks to Jesus

Jesus took Peter, James, and John up a mountain to pray.

Jesus grew brighter and brighter until even his clothes shone dazzling white. The friends were amazed. Even Moses and Elijah, two of God's prophets from long ago, were there talking with Jesus!

Suddenly a misty cloud came down and they heard God say, "This is my Son. Listen to him!"

The kind stranger

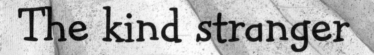

Jesus told another story:
A man was lying badly hurt
by the side of the road.

A priest came along.
But he did not help,
he just walked away!

Then another important man walked
by. But he did not stop to help either.

At last, a kind stranger stopped.
He bandaged the man, took him to
an inn, and looked after him there.

"Be kind like that stranger in
the story," said Jesus.

Martha and Mary

Jesus was at Martha and Mary's house.
Mary sat down to listen to Jesus.
But Martha rushed around getting
the food ready.

Martha was upset. "Jesus!" she said. "I'm doing all the work by myself. Tell Mary to help me!"

"Oh, Martha," said Jesus gently, "Mary wants to be with me. She has chosen what is most important."

A prayer to God

"Jesus, teach us how to talk to God," his friends asked.

So Jesus taught them this prayer:

Our Father in heaven,
may everyone know and love you.
Come and be our King.
Give us today the food we need.
Forgive the bad things we do.
Help us to forgive others too.
When we want to do
something bad, help
us choose to do
good instead.

Saying thank you

One day Jesus met some men with a skin disease. "Jesus, please make us better!" they called.

"Find the priest," Jesus said kindly, "so he can see you are well again."

As the men set off, they saw that their skin was as good as new! But only one of them rushed back to thank Jesus.

The party

"God invites people into his kingdom," Jesus said, "like the man who was getting ready for his party."

"The important people he had invited sent messages saying, 'We're sorry, we're too busy to come.'

"Then the man told his servants, 'Go! Find the people who are never invited to parties and bring them here.' Soon the man's house was full of people having fun."

The lost sheep

Everyone crowded around as Jesus told thi story about what God's kingdom is like:

There was once a shepherd who had one hundred sheep. One day he discovered one was missing.

He searched up and down, near and far. Finally he found it. He was so happy he carried it all the way home!

"I've found my lost sheep!" he called to his friends. "Let's have a party!"

Like the shepherd in the story, God is happy when even one sinner turns back to him.

Coming home

There was once a son who left home.
He soon spent his father's money.

"I'm hungry and unhappy," the young man thought.
"I'll go back and tell my father I'm sorry."

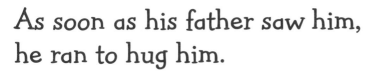

As soon as his father saw him,
he ran to hug him.

"My son has come home!"
he called to his servants.
"Let's have a party!"

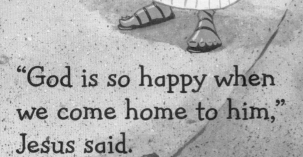

"God is so happy when
we come home to him,"
Jesus said.

Please forgive me!

Two men went to the temple to pray.

The first man said, "God, I keep all your rules, I don't cheat or steal like that man there."

The second man stood sadly at the back. "I know I'm a bad man, God." He prayed, "Please forgive me."

"Guess which man God was pleased with?" said Jesus. "The one who said he was sorry."

Jesus gives new life

Martha and Mary were very sad because their brother Lazarus had died.

"I can give new life," Jesus said to them. "Anyone who trusts me will never really die."

He went to the place where
Lazarus was buried.

"Move the stone away!" Jesus ordered.
"Lazarus, come out!" he called.

And to everyone's amazement,
Lazarus walked out alive and well.

John 11

Jesus and the children

Some people brought their children to see Jesus but Jesus' friends said, "Go away! Don't bother Jesus. He's much too busy."

Jesus was angry with them.

"Let the children come to me," he said. "Don't stop them. God wants children in his kingdom." The children ran to Jesus' open arms. He hugged them and asked God to take special care of them.

Mark 10

Zacchaeus changes

"I can't see Jesus over this crowd," thought Zacchaeus, so he climbed a tree.

Jesus walked by and looked up. "Hello, Zacchaeus!" he said. "I'm coming to your house today!"

The crowd gasped. Zacchaeus was a cheat; nobody liked him! Zacchaeus gasped. Could Jesus really want to be his friend?

Zacchaeus had a wonderful day with Jesus. And he promised not to cheat anyone again.

Luke 19

Expensive perfume

As Jesus and his friends were eating, Mary poured her precious bottle of perfume over Jesus' feet. Then she wiped them gently with her long hair.

The wonderful, sweet smell filled the room.

"Mary should have sold that perfume and given the money to the poor," complained Judas.

But Jesus was pleased with Mary. "Mary has done something very special for me!" he said.

Entering Jerusalem

Jesus rode into Jerusalem on a young donkey. The people spread branches and cloaks on the ground—like a carpet for a king.

The crowds waved branches
to welcome Jesus.

"Hooray for God's special king!" they
cheered. "Who is this man?" people asked.
"It's Jesus! God's messenger!"
the crowds replied.

Being ready

"Be ready for God's kingdom," said Jesus, as he told this story:

There were ten bridesmaids who were waiting for the bridegroom to arrive.

The wise girls took
extra oil for their
lamps. The foolish
girls did not. At
midnight their lamps ran out of oil,
so they went off to buy more.

Suddenly, the bridegroom arrived. He took
the wise bridesmaids to his wedding party.
But the foolish bridesmaids missed out.

Matthew 25

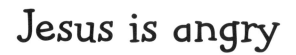

Jesus is angry

God's temple was busy
when Jesus arrived.

"Buy a lamb here," shouted some sellers.
"Doves for sale!" yelled others.

Jesus was very angry. There was so
much noise; no one could talk to God.

"God's house is a special place to pray," said Jesus, pushing over a stall piled high with money, "not somewhere to buy and sell and cheat!" Then he chased them all out of the temple.

Mark 11

Washing feet

One evening, during supper, Jesus got up, tied a towel around his waist, and began to wash his friends' feet.

They were shocked— it was the servant's job to wash feet.

"Jesus, you mustn't wash our feet!" said Peter.

"I'm washing your feet because I love you," said Jesus. "Now copy me. Love and help each other."

A special meal

Jesus was eating a special meal with his friends when he took some bread, thanked God, broke it in pieces, and handed it around.

"This is my body," he said. "I give it for you." Then he took a cup of wine, thanked God, and passed it around.

"Drink this," he said. "I will die for many people because God has promised to forgive them."

Matthew 26

Jesus is taken prisoner

Jesus was praying in the garden. He was sad because he knew he was going to die soon.

"Father, don't let me die," he prayed. "But if dying is part of your plan then I will do what you want."

Suddenly Jesus' friend Judas arrived, leading a crowd of Jesus' enemies!

He kissed Jesus. At once the soldiers surrounded Jesus and took him prisoner.

Peter lets Jesus down

Peter followed Jesus
and the soldiers.
"Aren't you Jesus'
friend?" asked a servant girl.

Peter shook his head. "No! I don't know him!"

Two more people asked if he knew Jesus. "No!" said Peter. "No!"

Suddenly a rooster crowed. Peter remembered that Jesus had said: "Before the rooster crows, you will say three times that you're not my friend." Peter burst into tears.

Jesus is left to die

Jesus' enemies took Jesus to Pilate, the Roman ruler. Pilate asked Jesus lots of questions. Then he said, "Jesus has not done anything wrong. I will let him go."

"NO!" the people shouted. "Kill Jesus! Nail him to a cross!"

So Pilate's soldiers nailed Jesus to a cross and left him to die.

Jesus knew that he had done what God wanted. "My work is finished!" he cried. Then he died.

John 18–19

221

A sad day

Jesus was dead. Nicodemus and Joseph of Arimathea had been afraid to say they were Jesus' friends.

But now they showed that they loved him. They wrapped Jesus' body in cloth with precious perfumes and carefully put him in a new tomb.

Together they rolled the heavy stone across the doorway. Then they walked sadly away.

John 19

Jesus is alive!

Two days later, Mary Magdalene stood outside Jesus' tomb. It was empty! Jesus' body was gone!

"Why are you crying?" asked a man standing nearby. "Have you taken Jesus away?" Mary sobbed.

"Mary!" said the man gently. Mary looked up. It was Jesus! He smiled. "Go and tell my friends."

Mary ran all the way. She couldn't wait to tell them the good news—Jesus was ALIVE!

John 20

A surprise

Two of Jesus' friends met a man on their way home.

"Jesus was killed three days ago," they told him, "but Mary says Jesus is alive again!"

"God promised this would happen to his special king," said the stranger.

At supper time, the man thanked God for the bread, then gave it to the friends. Suddenly the friends knew—the stranger was Jesus. He really was alive!

Luke 24

Tell everyone!

The two friends ran back to Jerusalem. "We've seen Jesus!" they said to all of Jesus' friends.

Suddenly Jesus was there too! Everyone stopped talking.

"Don't be scared," Jesus said. "It's me. Touch me—I'm not a ghost!"

They were so happy to
see Jesus alive again.

"Tell everyone everywhere about me,"
Jesus told them. "Because of me, they can
be God's friends again."

Luke 24

Thomas believes

Thomas didn't believe Jesus was alive. "When I have seen and touched Jesus for myself, then I'll believe," he said.

A week later, Jesus came again.
"Thomas, look! Touch my hands and feet.
It really is me," Jesus said.

Thomas gazed at him.
"My Lord and my God!" he said.

"Now you believe!" said Jesus.
"God is pleased with people who
believe even if they don't see me."

John 20

Jesus goes to heaven

"Wait in Jerusalem," Jesus told his friends. "God will send you his Holy Spirit. He will help you tell the whole world about me."

Then, before their eyes, Jesus was taken up to heaven.

Suddenly two men dressed in white appeared.

"Why are you standing here looking at the sky?" they asked. "Jesus will come back one day."

Acts 1

233

The Holy Spirit

Jesus' friends were praying when . . .
Whoosh! A sound like a rushing wind
roared through
the house.

A flickering flame rested gently on
each head. God's Holy Spirit had come
to help them tell others about Jesus.

When the people from other countries heard what God had done, they wanted to be Jesus' friends too.

A man walks again

Peter and John were going to the temple.

"Please give me money!" begged a man who could not walk.
"I don't have any," Peter said kindly, "but I know Jesus, God's king. And Jesus tells you to walk!"

Right away the man's feet and legs
were strong again—he could walk,
run, and jump! "Thank you!" he shouted.
"God is great!"

An important man

God's angel sent Philip to a dusty desert road. The chariot of an important African man rumbled by.

"Keep up with that chariot, Philip," said God's Holy Spirit.

Philip ran alongside. He heard the man reading God's book. "Do you understand it?" asked Philip.

"No," sighed the man. "What does it mean?"

Philip explained that it was all about Jesus, and the man decided to become Jesus' friend too.

Acts 8

239

Jesus speaks to Paul

Paul did not believe that Jesus was God's special king. He hated Jesus' friends.

He set off to find them and put them in prison.

FLASH! A bright light shone. Paul fell to the ground.

"Paul, why do you hate me and hurt me?" said a voice.

"Who are you?"
asked Paul.
"I am Jesus!"

Paul was shocked. Jesus was alive!
From that moment Paul became Jesus' friend.
"Go and tell everyone about me," Jesus said.

Acts 9

God rescues Peter

Peter was in prison. The soldiers guarded him night and day. One night an angel shook Peter awake. Peter's chains fell to the ground.

"Quick, put on your sandals," said the angel. "Follow me."

So Peter followed the angel past the guards, through the gate, and into the street. Then the angel disappeared.

Peter blinked. It wasn't a dream—he really was free!

Friends of Jesus

Paul traveled to many places telling people about Jesus.

One night a man called to Paul in a dream, "Come to Macedonia! Help us!"

The next day Paul sailed to Macedonia.

There he met Lydia, a rich woman, and
her friends. He told them about Jesus.
So Lydia and her friends became friends
of Jesus too.

Paul is taken prisoner

One day, when Paul was at the temple,
Jesus' enemies tried to kill him.
"Paul tells lies!" they shouted.

Just then the Roman commander
marched in. His soldiers stopped the
people from hurting Paul.

Paul explained that God wanted everyone to know Jesus was alive, but the crowd shouted, "NO! Get rid of Paul."

So the commander put Paul in prison.

Acts 21, 22

God keeps his promise

"The Roman emperor must decide if I am right," Paul said.

So the soldiers took Paul and set sail for Rome. Before long the ship was caught in a raging storm.

"Don't be afraid," said Paul.
"God will keep us all safe."

As the ship broke up, everyone swam
for the shore. At last they reached the
land—cold, wet, but safe.

God had kept
his promise.

Acts 27

Letters from Paul

Finally Paul and the soldiers arrived in Rome.

Paul was still a prisoner, but he was allowed to write to all the people he had met on his travels. They had become friends of Jesus too.

They told Paul their problems and he wrote back to help them.
"Keep on loving Jesus," Paul wrote, "and keep on loving each other."

A new heaven and earth

One day John saw a man—strong, good, and shining bright. It was Jesus!

"Write to my friends," Jesus said. "Tell them that God is going to make a new heaven and a new earth where no one will be hurt or die! All God's friends will live with him forever."

Index

This index shows where to find some favorite Bible stories in this book and also shows groups of stories that link together.

The New Testament

255

First mention of people in this book